The Honey Bun Thief

by Katie Dale
illustrated by Alette Straathof

OXFORD
UNIVERSITY PRESS

Each Monday, Nelson and Musa's mother baked honey buns. She sold them at the market. One day, she put a dozen on the garden table to cool.

Soon, a bun went missing.

"Who took one of my lovely honey buns?" called their mother.

"Musa must have because I didn't!" said Nelson.

Their mother was cross.

"Don't squabble!" she said.

The brothers gave each other a glare as they went inside.

From the window, they saw a wild monkey.
It crept down from a tree ...

The monkey took a honey bun and ran off!

“Hey!” shouted Nelson.

“So the monkey is the thief,” said Musa.

The monkey snatched another bun as the boys ran outside.

"How can we protect the honey buns?" asked Nelson.

"We cannot keep watch all day," said Musa.

"I have a clever scheme!" said Musa.

He looked pleased with himself. He covered the buns with a big basket.

Yet when they went inside, the monkey knocked it off. It took another bun!

"It didn't work!" moaned Musa.

“I have a plan!” said Nelson.

He covered the buns with the basket again. Then he walked to a boulder close by.

"Help me with this," called Nelson. "This will weigh the basket down."

The boys placed the heavy boulder on top.

All day long, the monkey tried to shift the boulder. It could not do it!

"Great!" cried Nelson.

The monkey looked sad as it leaped into its tree. Hidden behind a branch was the monkey's tiny baby.

"She's a mother!" gasped Nelson.

"I wonder if her baby is hungry?" asked Musa.

"We can't give her another bun," said Nelson.

"No, but we can't let them go hungry," said Musa.

Musa pointed at a fig tree.

“Monkeys like to eat fig buds,” he said.

“How can we help her find the tree?” said Nelson.

“I have an idea!” cried Musa.

He fetched a bud from the fig tree. He tossed it to the mother monkey. It landed in front of her.

At first, the mother monkey did not see the bud.
The boys were disappointed.

Slowly, the mother monkey got down from the tree. She sniffed at the fig bud. Then she began to eat it.

Excited, the brothers left a trail of fig buds. The mother monkey followed the trail. The baby was on her shoulders.

"It worked!" exclaimed Musa, grinning with relief.

"Look, the monkeys are with their friends," said Nelson. "They will spread the seeds so new fig trees grow."

When their mother saw the buns, she was crosser than ever. She pointed at the table.

“Now there are only eight buns left!” she declared.

Musa told their mother about the monkeys and the buns. Nelson told her about the fig tree.

“I’m so proud of you both,” she said.

A batch of freshly baked honey buns appeared.

"You each deserve a honey bun!" their mother said.

Look Back

Encourage students to use the pictures to retell the story.